# Elixir

Sabika Saiyed

BookLeaf Publishing

India | USA | UK

Presentation by *BookLeaf Publishing*

Web: www.bookleafpub.com

E-mail: info@bookleafpub.com


ISBN: 9789363310865

First edition 2024

*This book is dedicated firstly to the Almighty and His chosen Divine Leaders, who gave me the strength to face all the challenges life came up with and who gave me patience in times of overwhelming uncertainty. I can never be thankful enough to them for all the blessings they showered upon me. All praise and glory belong to them.*

*And secondly, to my parents, who are my strongest support and greatest inspiration and who bring life to my life. My Nana, a pure-hearted, selfless man of wisdom, who loved his children and grandchildren dearly. To my beautiful friends who stayed with me through thick and thin and loved me despite my flaws.*

# ACKNOWLEDGEMENT

I am really grateful to my dearest caring brother and friend, Dr. Mrudul Bhatjiwale, for his valuable input and help.
I am especially thankful to BookLeaf Publishing for providing such a wonderful platform and helping me share my thoughts with the world.

# PREFACE

Unpredictability is the norm of life, and the one thing I can affirmatively state is that times always change. Accepting my situation while trying to move forward and working on improving myself has been my key to mental peace.

There were times when I yearned for someone to share my thoughts with and vent my emotions; times when I was alone, when no one understood me; in these moments, my feelings and emotions overwhelmed me. In that solitude, I began penning down my thoughts, and it has been one of the best decisions of my life. The feelings that I thought would otherwise lead to an implosion now found a beautiful and productive escape.

Each poem is a result of intense emotions, a smooth blend of my feelings and memories. These compositions helped me process my emotions, face them, feel them, deal with them, and heal from them.

Having albinism and being different was not always easy. What shapes the thinking of a child are the lessons learned from teachers and peers, with whom they closely interact throughout their development, of which compassion plays a major role. Every inch of me wishes and hopes that people would become more compassionate towards those who are different from them.

Everything I am today, despite the odds, I owe to my parents. I am a physiotherapist with a postgraduate degree and a fellowship, and moreover, someone who now understands her worth. I am not infallible, I am not perfect, I am not everything you wish I were, but I am me.

On that note, I hope you like these compositions, and I hope you connect with them.

# Confession

I see my long-lost love,

standing before me

and my mind

drifts back to the past

when I had so many opportunities

to confess my feelings for you,

before it was too late.

But regretfully, I didn't.

I wish I told you I loved you,

when it was time.

When your eyes wandered

to search for assurance,

I wish I told you

that you are enough

that your efforts won't go in vain.

I love you.

When you wished for a friend,

I wish I told you

that you are so strong

you possess such strength

you are your best friend.

That in you

I see a wonderful human,

with a beautiful heart

I love you.

When you second-guessed your hard work,

I wish I told you

that you create masterpieces.

You fare great.

When you write,

your heart spills out the purity

and the pain

as you want it to show.

I love you.

When you yearned for acceptance,

I wish I told you

my love for you

outshines everyone else's.

That you radiate love, yourself.

I love you.

When you cried,

I wish I had wiped your tears

given you a tight hug

and made you smile.

Because that smile is your strongest asset.

I love you.

When you lost confidence in yourself,

I wish I had talked to you time and again

about your perseverance and achievements.

About giving yourself some credit

and loving yourself.

I love you.

How I wish that I told you these things

when the time was right.

Now years have passed

and such a long time has slipped away.

Like sand slipping away

from beneath my feet

as the tide forces it back

into the ocean.

It's late now.

But not too late, I guess.

I've finally accepted

my feelings for you.

I can't stay in denial now.

I have to let the world know

what my heart feels.

So, my love,

I finally say it.

Out loud and with pride

before the entire world,

I love you!

Saying that I smile

with a little tear of joy in my eyes

and a lump in my throat.

I smile wide.

And turn away from the mirror.

# The brightly shining future!

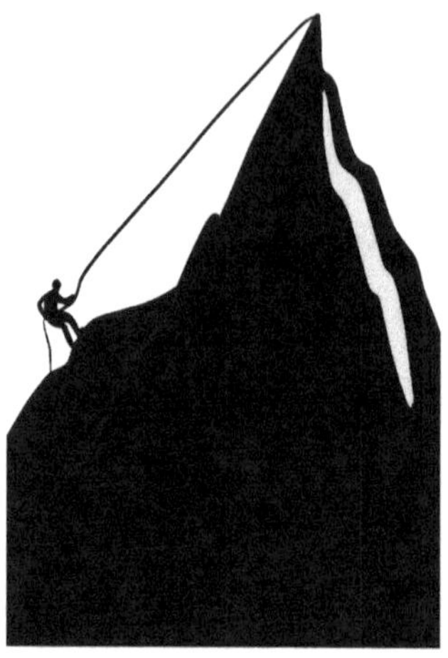

A step towards

the shining light,

Is all you need

to make things right.


You think you're weak

your spirit is broken.

Is it really true though?

Huge skies you've shaken!

You faced all lows

and still came through.

Don't you notice

the strength in you?


Remember the time,

you thought you'd quit.

With whatever you had

you gave every bit.


The world wasn't fair

You were damaged, in pain.

Yet you strove hard

thought of others' gain.


Remember that time

When you had no one.

Your best friends were then,

your grit and devotion.

So why tremble now,

Why doubt, why fear?

Step up, work hard

for your next endeavor.


You're filled with love,

valor, foresight.

Take a step dear,

towards the shining light.

# Chevalier

You're a hero!

When you wipe your own tears,

when you hold yourself together,

keeping your mind sane

and your priorities straight,

crying in solitude

but not giving up.

Cruising through the storm

of pain and hurt,

moving on,

keeping faith in the Almighty.

Remember,

your tears are not your weakness.

They're the mirror of your soul.

Strong and courageous!

Therefore, believe it entirely,

however little or insignificant you may feel,

It isn't perpetual.

By His grace,

you are, and will always be,

a hero!

# Tranquil grace

Have you ever wondered who you are,

what you feel, what you think?

Have you ever come face to face with a conflict,

of your own identity, of your own self?

A feeling so strong, so consuming

It cages you,

from where you feel there is no escape;

You crave answers and yearn for confirmation.

and yet the only person who can give you that,

is your own confused self.

Is ignorance bliss? You wonder,

What would it be like, had you never had these questions,

to begin with,

Then you look around and

you find people not seeking out the answers,

to the questions from their hearts, from within their souls.

Unaware of their conduct, oblivious to their deeds.

People, not willing to introspect, avoiding facing themselves.

and you also see the adjustments

their loved ones have to make.

You see how they have influenced others' lives

by dwelling in the dark.

Being brutally insensitive

to the existence of the lives

of those with broken hearts surrounding them.

And then you become thankful

for the painful war inside you.

Which is excruciating, scary, and confusing.

But it is only so to you.

# Life – a beautiful paradox

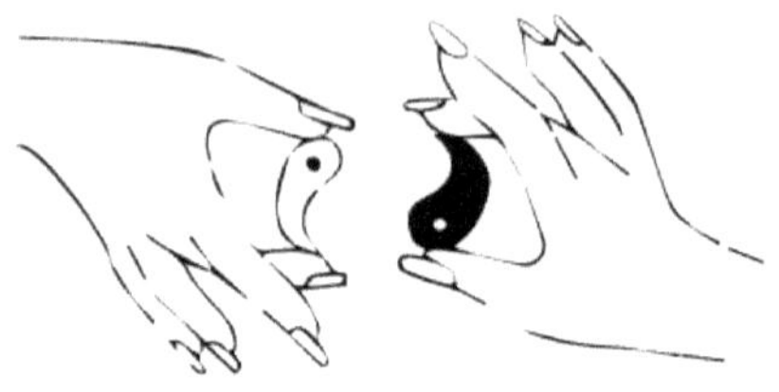

Above the scorching, heated land
I feel the cool breeze where I stand.

Upon the thorny path I walk
I also feel the softest flock.

The pricks of pointy thorns I sense
Though flowers come for my defense.

Along the bad and hurt and pain,
Comes also glory, love, and gain.

So, this is life, what I have seen
In darkness lies a beauty, serene.

Don't you ever go in despair
Accept it all, what is out there.

So, take the good, the bad, the best
And God will take care of the rest.

# Welcome to the future!

You know you've grown up

when you're no longer defensive.

When you no longer search

for people to be there for you.

Realizing it's only you

who must fight for yourself.

When you're less anxious

about unforeseen happenings.

When the pain of loved ones

becomes more important

And your health and joy

take a backseat.

When the list of those whom you share your
pain with

becomes even smaller.

When you become more selective

about who sees your tears fall.

When what matters most

is your own view of yourself

And others' opinions

hold no value unless they help you grow.

When the only one you wish to please

is the Almighty.

Remember when you were young?

You dreamed of growing up.

but now, after all the exams you've faced,

you realize growing up has a deeper meaning.

It is when you've reached

the ever-evolving phase

of self-love and enlightenment,

you know you've grown up.

Welcome to where you always wanted to be!

and if you're not happy right now,

if you're not satisfied yet,

you haven't reached your destination.

Keep walking!

# And life goes on

Walking on the ashes,

the remains of what's left,

the dust, the smoke,

I can see what's left behind.

It's all visible now.

The destruction, the pain,

and even though it hurts like hell.

Walking on the sharp, broken pieces

of my once broken soul,

I feel gratitude and a deep sense of relief.

and I smile with my heart.

My eyes twinkle with the tears of pride

on how I handled the storm.

Amused by my resilience

and proud of my determination.

Blessed by the Almighty.

Wounded and in pain,

I still continue to move forward,

and past the remains of what was left.

To build a new world, AGAIN!

# Smile

Stay strong, don't cry,
Let it build up as the times fly.

Let them come to you, let them speak,
They need you now, you can't go weak.

You cannot cry, you cannot whine,
Hide those dark clouds behind the fake sunshine.

Your tears need to hide, your secrets veiled,
Hold yourself strong behind a shield.

Your faith, family, friends, the loves of your life,
Their love is the reason, keeping you alive.

Hold on, hold it in, let it all sink in,
These tears will one day find their escape from
within.

# The gentle savage

She'll care, she'll love,

She'll stay, be a friend,

With her shield of prayers,

Holding on till the end.


She will hide her pain,

Keeping it out of sight,

With a smile for a mask,

Doing everything that's right.


Such is a woman,

A beacon of love,

As brave as a lioness,

As tender as a dove.


But dearest to her is

Her honor, her pride.

A lady raised well

Will never let that hide.


Her silence is patience,

Her firmness is care.

Don't take it for granted;

Don't you ever dare!


With all her might,

She'll fiercely defend

Her pride, her dignity

Until the end.


So don't you test her;

You will pay the cost.

Her love, her care, her trust

Will forever be lost.

# Masquerade

It starts slowly,

a darkness surrounds you.

Pouring out your emotions,

letting your tears out

makes you feel better.

And then,

it happens all over again.

Negativity, anxiety, and fear surround you.

You once again look around

to find that shoulder

on which you can lean and cry.

Once again, you let down your defenses,

Speak up, share, wail, lament.

And then again, you feel better.

but this is continuous,

hauntingly repetitive,

like an unending maze.

You don't know how much of it

is going to consume you.

Having no idea

of what will remain of you

when all this ends,

Or if it ever will.

You keep on anticipating

another dark moment,

hoping it never comes.

And if it does, you'll go back

To those who would take a sip

of your tears and yet

smile back at you.

But they too have hearts.

They too have needs.

Your constant need for

support has drained them.

Your vacuum of sadness has

sucked their strength.

And before you realize,

you've unknowingly changed their world.

You didn't want that.

But you did.

And now you look around

but find no one.

Although you are surrounded

with love and care,

Now,

you know that you are alone.

Then you realize that it's you

who should be strong enough,

because now you cannot cause

any more hurt.

So even if you are crying inside, you smile.

You still are anticipating

Negativity, anxiety, and fear.

but this time, you look for

A quiet place, a strategy, an escape,

which could make you feel lighter,

and not drag your loved ones

down with you.

So now you have a big smile,

because even you are tired

of relieving your burden

onto the selfless, caring souls.

And eventually,

it becomes your habit

of living with it.

You don't know when it will end.

The help that you need is consistent,

that even those with the best intentions

cannot keep up with it.

So now you fear every caring question.

You get alarmed

When you're asked, "Are you okay?"

and you find yourself with a

dilemma in your mind:

Should I tell the truth,

or should I just smile?

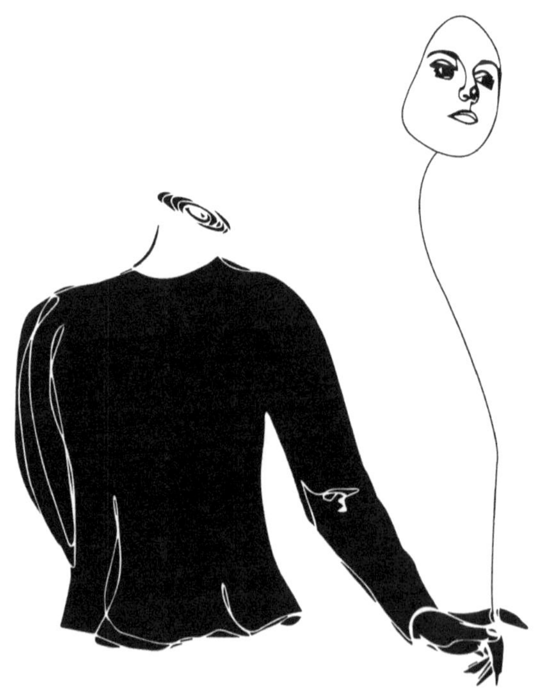

# Smiling captives

When we can confide in our only companion:
solitude.

When talking seems redundant.

When sharing your thoughts with your loved
ones seems difficult.

We accept the cage

of our ruminating thoughts

as our home, our safe place.

A place where we

are all by ourselves,

facing our scariest demons,

and eventually, inevitably, becoming accustomed
to them.

This becomes our reality, our new normal.

and that cage becomes our "home"

And we, its captives.

We refuse to open up,

or reach out for help.

Fearing about the pain that we might cause

our loved ones,

by sharing our fears,

burdening them with our anxiety,

and dragging them down with us,

into this emotional hell.

For this guilt is harder to endure,

than the pain caused by our own horrifying
thoughts and asphyxiating feelings.

So, we keep quiet, we cry in silence, we stride
on, we grow.

and in the process, we change!

Conditioning ourselves to survive and be there
to function,

as productive and positive members of society,

as pillars of support for those around us.

To give to others

what we never received, yearned, and hoped
deeply for.

Smiling, suppressing, and caging our demons
inside.

# Lemonade

Walking, wandering, strolling ahead,

with my destination in my mind,

I look at what I have earned,

I look at what I have learned.

With each obstacle in my way,

I've learned to strive harder.

I've learned that life

doesn't always go as planned.

With each harsh word

targeted towards me,

I've learned to be polite;

To not cause the pain that I have felt.

With each loved one parting ways,

I've learned to love more,

so that my friends

don't ever feel alone in my presence.

With each taunt that I have been struck with,

I've learned to not poke the sharp stick

where it hurts the most.

With each tear that I have shed,

I've learned to be there for others.

With each moment that I have spent alone,

I've learned that in solitude lies one's strength.

With each dark experience,

I've learned that I am surrounded by immense
love

of God, of my family, and of my friends.

It's okay to suffer,

It's good to feel pain,

For that pain then changes you.

It makes you stronger.

It makes you shine.

It teaches you to be human,

to love, respect, and help.

I've come to value happiness now,

I've learned to be grateful,

for all the support and care embracing me.

I have learned more than ever before!

For I've tasted the sweet and tangy sparkling
water of life!

So don't worry if life gives you lemons.

Make your lemonade,

And be liberal with the sugar!

# Beneath the surface

Don't you hear that agonizing silent cry?

Don't you see those eyes speaking volumes

of thousands of experiences?

Some good, some better, some bad, some worse.

That smile is probably concealing

an aching, sobbing heart.

That cheerful, confident personality

could be a shield

for a person hurting inside.

Everyone has a story to tell.

Everyone is going through something.

We may not be able to perceive it.

People mostly have their guards up.

So, let's decide

to never let anyone

feel hurt or offended.

At least individually,

let's try not to add to someone else's challenges.

Not everyone who is smiling is happy.

So, let's be kind, cordial, and compassionate.

To strengthen each other,

to make this world an easier place to live in.

Not everyone surrounded by people

feels a sense of belonging.

So, let's be polite, caring, and friendly.

To pull each other out of their misery.

So, this world feels like home

to every person residing here.

Not everyone who is talking

is speaking their hearts out.

So, let's be empathetic, attentive, and patient.

To make everyone feel

that there is an ear to listen.

Let's make it easy to reach out for help

to those who need it,

to rescue each other from despair.

Let's not assume that everyone

can handle the sharp wounds

of hurtful words and deceit.

Everyone is fighting a battle.

So let's be there.

Let's be a guiding light.

A non-judgmental,

and an unconditionally caring companion

to everyone.

Let's spread positivity.

Let's spread love.

# Enlightening anguish

I'm thankful for this silence;

it has made me more resilient.

Those words that were never spoken to me,

I know how to say them when someone is in need.

I know the value of hearing out,

I'll be a good listener to those who wish to share their pain.

That shoulder I didn't have to cry upon,

I'll provide it to a hurting soul.

I know just how important it is to be there for someone in pain.

I know the value of condolences,

of kind words, encouragement, and assurances.

I'll spread them as much as I can,

For I know their worth.

# Warriors of the untold battle

I feel for those,

who find themselves alone

in a crowded place.

Where faces seem familiar

but feelings don't.

I feel for those,

who say they're depressed.

Their racing hearts and emotions

are not always in their control.

I feel for those,

who don't have power over themselves

and explicitly, those having the insight of it!

How challenging it might be...

To be filled with the fear of being judged.

For the things that are out of their hands.

I feel for those who hear "cheer up," "think
positive," "be strong"!

When they know that they cannot

just switch their emotions on and off.

I feel for those,

with whom people brag about their difficult
lives,

and how they heroically coped with it.

With those who are already well accomplished,

but struck by a disease.

I feel for those...

They are the brave warriors!

The sensitive beings.

The motivated souls.

Who fights back

silently.

Even when they are drowning in despair.

Even when they can't see the light.

Even when they can't judge the direction,

in which they should move.

But they persevere,

Keep struggling

To stay calm,

To stay composed,

To stay functional,

for their God, their family, their friends, and
themselves,

even while struggling with their own identities.

Battling their demons.

These warriors are special!

They understand more,

they judge less,

they are empathetic.

Because they have witnessed those phases of
life,

which not everyone is blessed to have been
through!

Fighting the war within themselves.

A difficult war

not meant for the weak!

So, let's encourage them

and at least try to learn

how to be and how to act,

and what to say,

while being around those who need care.

So that their journey becomes easier.

And we don't keep dragging them

back to where they had moved forward from.

So that they could heal.

And we could have the opportunity

to make a positive impact

In someone's life!

# A healing embrace

A tender touch of love

And a pleasing smile

Can make someone feel wanted

Lend others time awhile.


A little more respect than

What others would expect

Could melt the hardened hearts

Of souls depressed and wrecked.


A moment of your time,

A gift of your presence,

Could wipe a trail of tears,

Off of a saddened face.

A little act of kindness,

A gentle hand of care,

And some words of concern,

Is all you need to share.


It's not that tough, believe me

It is quite possible!

Make this world worth living,

It's all up to your will.

# Be kind

The stench of filthy words remains,

The sting of curses stays.

The world is already so glum,

Just work in kinder ways.


What all you say might scar a soul,

Might break one's self-esteem.

Just 'cause you had an awful day,

It's not okay to SCREAM!

You want to let off steam, I know

I see it pertinent.

But passing on your pain and hurt,

Is that the way to vent?


Let others also have a voice.

Let them feel understood.

Just practice being kinder

For every person's good.


Your bitter, hurtful, grimy words,

Your anger, lashing out

Might haunt someone's memory,

For years, day in, day out.


It isn't as gruelingly tough,

It doesn't take a dime.

Spread loads of love and happiness,

There's nothing more sublime!

# Ineffable thoughts

When all you hear

is the screeching of perplexing thoughts,

tearing apart the engulfing silence around you.

Thrashing your soul for the answers

to so many unanswered questions

raging through your mind.

It is in those moments

you find your strength.

In those moments

you feel grateful for your fortitude.

And proud of your stoicism.

The beauty here is

that this feeling is so profound.

And yet, you cannot place a finger

on exactly what it is,

You just feel.

Love, anger, glee, guilt,

sadness, contentment, joy, restlessness.

A feeling so voracious and insatiable.

You feel it all.

And even though it is overwhelming,

you are thankful, for at least

being blessed with the insight,

and being able to acknowledge

these ineffable thoughts.

# In search of a sunshine

I am walking on a gloomy boulevard,

and in the name of belongings to my name,

all I have

are the blessings of my loved ones, my experiences,

and a newly found skill of having self-love and faith.

Still difficult for me to put into practice.

I keep walking

with a hope

to get rid of the dark emptiness

that forces me to take each step.

I walk forward and keep striving.

Because I know that

at least towards the end of it,

I would have something to look back at.

A journey full of stories of hard work and
resilience.

A journey filled with love and compassion.

A journey of perseverance and patience.

A journey of never giving up!

And even if I don't find the light

with which I want to illuminate my world

I will still have the memories

of that beautiful journey I took

in search of a sunshine.

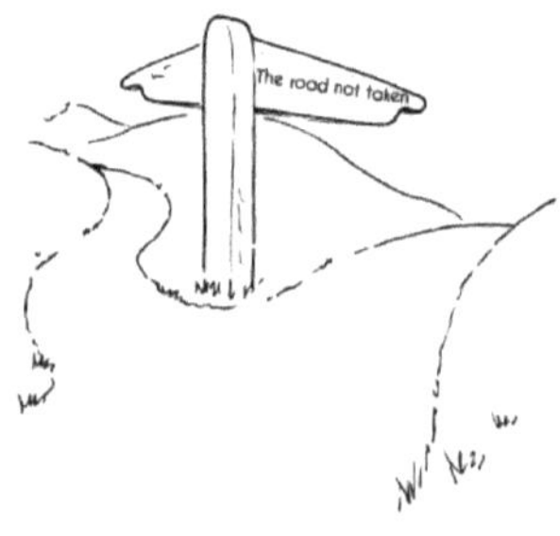

# Strange love

I'm lying to you,

And you can't see.

Perhaps you've lost

Your friend in me.


You see me smile,

You see me cheer.

My silent cries

You fail to hear.


I think of the days

You'd catch me when I lied.

Today you can't,

How hard I've tried!

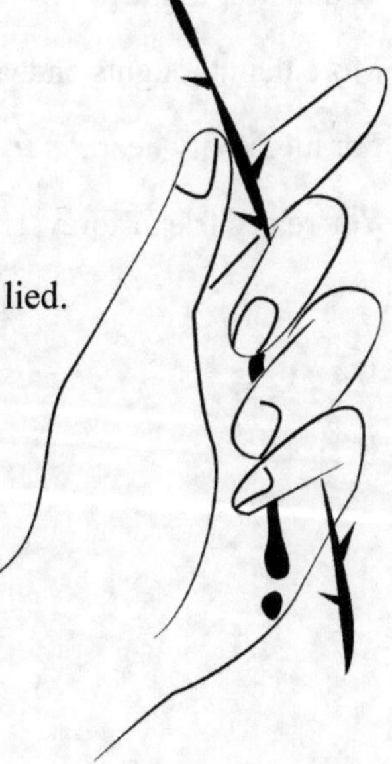

I love you, dear,

My friend, my relief.

Still, in your voice,

Vanishes my grief.


I have complaints,

Yet loads of love,

You are my angel

Sent from above!


You matter to me

More than thoughts endeavor.

For me, in my heart,

You're my friend forever!

# Blunted feelings

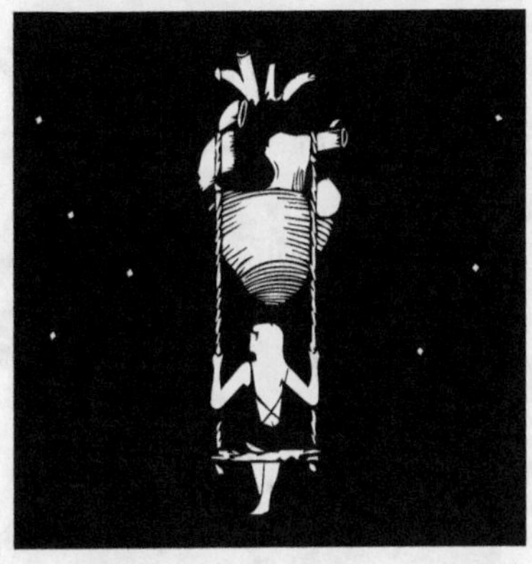

There were times

when my emotions

firmly held the halter

of my sorrows and happiness.

When every word once said to me

was engraved on my heart and my soul.

Forever making me attentive

to how they made me feel.

Never leaving my mind,

wandering in my thoughts.

Every grin, every cringe, every frown,

once, got me on an emotional roller coaster.

Making me overthink,

Ruminating for hours and hours

about what they meant.

How emotionally taxing it was,

for which I have no words.

But as life does,

it kept moving on.

And these experiences

found a permanent place

on the pages of the diary of my life.

And I continued to feel it

with the same excruciating, habitual intensity.

I kept feeling, kept hurting.

Until I gave it a thought.

I tried to introspect.

And maybe I found the cause of this
self-sabotage!

It was the unnecessary expectations

from those whom I cared for.

and even from myself.

Thinking I would be able to deal

with everything that,

I would get myself into.

Without realizing, I haven't healed.

I haven't recovered,

from whatever that had changed me from within.

And that I actually wasn't ready

to give myself or anyone else a chance.

So, I held my heart

and persisted patiently.

Maybe my soul hardened,

or the blows of life got weaker,

I don't know.

Eventually, it started hurting less.

I'm not sad or sorry

Nor do I harbor regrets.

I don't feel happy, upset, or anything

on the fact that

It hurts a little less now.

It's just a fact; that's what it is.

So now, when those whom I loved,

seem far away.

Or when my fears make it hard to trust anyone,

or when my naivety makes me love someone I
shouldn't,

And then I get stabbed in the back,

I hurt a lot less now.

I am not seeking the answer to the question

of whether I've become strong or given up or
matured,

or I've been too hurt to feel any pain.

This is me now,

at that I shall leave it.

# A hidden universe

That which is glowing could be burning inside.
Articulate and expressive but emotions that hide.

Quiet and lonely to you she may seem,
Perhaps she's nurturing a beautiful dream?

Your eyes only see what lies before you,
Remember, there's more beneath it too!

A volume of feelings one's heart can hold.
So don't be too quick to dismiss what is told.

Both a smile and a tear have a lot to convey.
Just try to acknowledge what comes your way.

Maybe you'll let down your guards of defense,
When you try to see the world through her lens.

Respect, regard, and concede, if need be,
Break the shackles of prejudices, let your mind
be free.

# Let there be light

The sun is black

it is burning inside.

Radiant and generous,

sharing its light.

Hiding itself very well

behind the burning flames,

so people see its light

And are blinded.

It continues to give

its loving warmth.

So that everything goes on

as it should.

It would rain,

the crops will grow,

the fields will wave,

with the blowing wind,

the birds will sing.

All living beings would survive.

All of this though

comes with a heavy cost.

The sun has to burn

Within its flames!

# Liberation

The more you don't care,

the stronger I become.

You ignore the signs of cries for help,

I'll harden.


I won't regret the friendship we had,

the memories we made,

the trust I once placed in you.


I will become numb.

Silent, observant, and aware.

I'll just keep on building a thicker wall around
me.

I'll refuse to give in thereafter,

to strike up a conversation.

So that I don't have to blame you.

For knowing and yet not helping.

Your innocence will forever stay fresh in my
heart.


I would still be the same.

I'd laugh the same,

talk the same, love the same.

I just wouldn't trust you

with my emotions, my secrets.


You'd always have a friend,

a secret keeper,

But not the one who shares.

Not the one expecting help.

I'll adapt and move on.

I'll refuse to give up

I'll strive harder,

on finding my happiness.


Though this time,

You won't be a part of that journey.

# Inevitable

We strive to be happy,

but often, we fail.

No one can dodge pain.

It touches every soul.

And yet, we give our all,

to run away from it.

Chasing an unrealistic desire,

an extraordinary expectation.

We need to learn to let ourselves cry.

Let ourselves feel the pain.

Let ourselves experience the agony.

Without getting overwhelmed,

and without letting the pain consume us.


We need to master the skill

of letting ourselves feel

whatever it is that we are feeling.

Without it entirely engulfing us.

Just taking it all in our stride,

moving on while feeling the pain.

Doing justice to all our responsibilities.


Because, in the end,

although inevitable, it isn't perpetual.

And the Almighty

is forever merciful.

# Tenacity

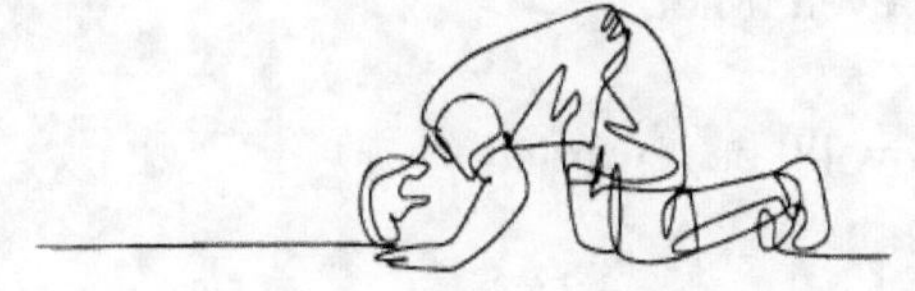

My heart continues to beat

through this pain, too intense.

Dragging myself forward

through a wait too long.

And when I lose hope,

I remind myself

that I am living the answers

to so many of my prayers.

Patiently waiting

while the world moves on.

He'll bless me someday.

My prayers will be heard.

And even if not,

I know I'll be rewarded,

albeit, just for praying!

Such is His graciousness.

I just have to be.

I just have to wait

for the answers from Him.

Cry through the pain,

laugh through the tears,

sleep through the inconveniences,

and smile through the agony.

And wait for His plans to unveil.

While I continue to seek

His response to my plea.

# A lesson well learned

I'm surprised, pleasantly.

Noticing how His plans work.

Realizing that His mercy holds no bounds.

Finally understanding why it happened, what
happened.

I've realised now that my tears of despair

Were a sign of my weak faith.

For this, I feel ashamed

but grateful

for the lessons I have learned.

It's difficult to express in words

what I am feeling inside.

All I know is that I've grown up!

He helped me,

He pushed me,

with His discipline and His love!

He saw me struggling and got me out of my misery,

making me more than what I had been before.

Life still mortifies me,

still stuns me,

amazes me.

And I wait, and I wait

For His plans to unveil!

www.ingramcontent.com/pod-product-compliance
Lightning Source LLC
LaVergne TN
LVHW011044200726
843509LV00011B/1350